REMARKABLE
PEOPLE

Justin
Bieber

by Anita Yasuda

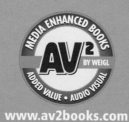

www.av2books.com

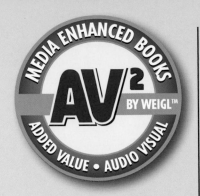

AV² provides enriched content that supplements and complements this book. Weigl's AV² books strive to create inspired learning and engage young minds in a total learning experience.

Your AV² Media Enhanced books come alive with...

Audio
Listen to sections of the book read aloud.

Key Words
Study vocabulary, and complete a matching word activity.

Video
Watch informative video clips.

Quizzes
Test your knowledge.

Embedded Weblinks
Gain additional information for research.

Slide Show
View images and captions, and prepare a presentation.

Try This!
Complete activities and hands-on experiments.

... and much, much more!

Go to **www.av2books.com**, and enter this book's unique code.

BOOK CODE

T805918

AV² by Weigl brings you media enhanced books that support active learning.

Published by AV² by Weigl
350 5th Avenue, 59th Floor
New York, NY 10118

www.av2books.com   www.weigl.com

Library of Congress Cataloging-in-Publication Data

Yasuda, Anita.
 Justin Bieber / Anita Yasuda.
    p. cm. -- (Remarkable people)
 Includes index.
 ISBN 978-1-61690-667-2 (hardcover : alk. paper) -- ISBN 978-1-61690-672-6 (softcover : alk. paper)
 1. Bieber, Justin, 1994---Juvenile literature. 2. Singers--Canada--Biography--Juvenile literature. I. Title.
 ML3930.B416Y37 2011
 782.42164092--dc22
 [B]
                              2010051002

Printed in the United States of American in North Mankato, Minnesota
5 6 7 8 9 0 16 15 14 13 12

WEP291112
112012

Editor: Heather Kissock
Design: Terry Paulhus

Photograph Credits
Weigl acknowledges Getty Images as the primary image supplier for this title.

Every reasonable effort has been made to trace ownership and to obtain permission to reprint copyright material. The publishers would be pleased to have any errors or omissions brought to their attention so that they may be corrected in subsequent printings.

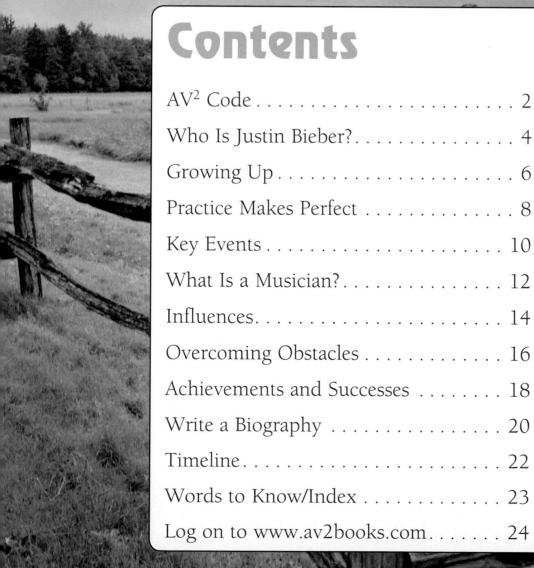

Contents

Who Is Justin Bieber?

Justin Bieber has risen from being the star of YouTube videos to an international singing sensation in only a few short years. When he was 12 years old, his mother began posting videos of Justin singing on YouTube for family and friends to see. A music industry **executive** found the videos, and the rest is history.

Three years later, in 2009, Justin's first **album** was released. Entitled My World, it debuted at number six on the **Billboard** charts. This was the highest opening release by a new artist at the time. The album sold more than 137,000 copies in its first week.

Since then, Justin's popularity has soared. He has performed for President Barack Obama at the White House, headlined a world tour, and embarked on an acting career. All of this was accomplished by the time Justin was 16 years old.

"I'm looking forward to influencing others in a positive way. My message is you can do anything if you just put your mind to it."

Growing Up

Justin Bieber was born on March 1, 1994. He grew up in Stratford, Ontario, Canada, a town of 30,000 people. After his parents divorced, Justin was raised by his mother Pattie Mallette. His father, Jeremy Bieber, remarried, and Justin now has two half-siblings, Jazmyn and Jaxon.

Growing up, Justin loved music. He was a natural performer who enjoyed playing **percussion**. Justin talks fondly of playing music on pots and pans in his family's kitchen. At the age of two, he started playing real drums.

Later, Justin taught himself to play piano and guitar. Before long, he was performing in public. Justin would sing for tourists outside a theater in Stratford.

Pattie often accompanies Justin to events such as awards shows.

Get to Know Ontario

FLOWER
White Trillium

TREE
Eastern
White Pine

BIRD
Loon

Toronto is the capital of Ontario. Ottawa, Canada's capital city, is located in Ontario as well.

Stratford, Ontario, is home to the largest Shakespeare festival in North America.

Ontario is the second-largest province in Canada. Only Quebec is larger.

More than 12 million people live in Ontario. This is about one third of Canada's population.

Think about it!

Celebrities such as Justin Bieber learn the pressures of being famous at a young age. Think about how your life would change if you became famous. Would you maintain previous friendships? Would it be easy to make new friends? Is there an everyday task you enjoy doing that you would no longer be able to do? What steps could you take to make your life as normal as possible?

Practice Makes Perfect

Even before he was old enough to go to school, Justin was singing and making music. One of Justin's first chances to sing professionally happened when he was still in public school.

Local Stratford vocal teacher, Jake Leiske, put together a Christmas CD to raise money for a local charity. Justin offered to sing on the title track, "Set a Place at Your Table." In support of the CD, Justin performed the song outside Stratford's city hall.

In 2007, when Justin was only 12 years old, he entered a local singing competition called Stratford Idol. Justin placed third, ahead of people who had been taking singing lessons. Though he did not win, Justin impressed the audience and judges.

■ Stratford Idol was patterned after *American Idol*, a U.S. television show. Country music star Carrie Underwood won the contest in 2005.

Justin's mother posted videos of him singing on YouTube for friends and family. More than 10 million people saw the videos. One of them was a music **agent** by the name of Scooter Braun. He contacted Justin and, over time, became his manager.

Scooter flew Justin to Atlanta, Georgia, to record **demos**. In Atlanta, Justin met **R&B** star Usher. Usher wanted to help Justin with his career. He arranged for Justin to meet with an executive from a major record company. Soon after, Justin signed his first recording contract.

Usher joined Justin on stage when he performed at New York's Madison Square Garden during his world tour.

Key Events

In the summer of 2009, Justin's first **single**, "One Time," came out. Three other songs, "One Less Lonely Girl," "Love Me," and "Favorite Girl," soon followed. Justin became the first solo artist to have four songs from a **debut** album in the Billboard Hot 100 before his album's release. When My World came out in November 2009, it quickly went **platinum** in the United States, selling more than one million copies.

Justin followed this album with My World 2.0. It debuted at number one on the Billboard charts. To support the album, Justin went on a major world tour in June 2010. The tour lasted six months, with Justin performing throughout North America and as far away as Japan.

In September 2010, Justin made his acting debut when he was a guest star on *CSI: Crime Scene Investigation*. More television appearances soon followed.

On *CSI: Crime Scene Investigation*, Justin played a troubled teen who was involved in a bombing.

Thoughts from Justin

Justin is grateful for the opportunities he has been given. Here are some of the comments he has made about touring, music, and life.

Justin talks about life on the road.

"I miss my friends, but other than that, I'm having a pretty good life traveling around the world, and just having fun."

Justin talks about touring.

"Being on the road is exhausting. It's fun, but at the same time it's... exhilarating."

Justin talks about keeping in touch with fans.

"...I think the Internet is the best way to reach your fans. A couple of years back, artists didn't have that tool, so why not use it now?"

Justin talks about how he wants his music to be received.

"I want them (fans) to hear my music and want to play it again because it made their hearts feel good."

Justin talks about his fast rise to fame.

"It's been pretty crazy coming from a little town in Canada and now being able to travel the world and do what I love."

Justin talks about his work ethic.

"The harder you work, the more successful you can be."

What Is a Musician?

A musician is a person who can play an instrument, sing, or write music. Some musicians, such as Justin Bieber, show they have a talent for music at a young age. It takes more than talent to work in the music industry, however. A musician must dedicate hours to improving his or her skills. Professional musicians spend hours practicing and rehearsing the music they play.

Most musicians specialize in a specific type of music, such as classical, jazz, or rock. They study for many years before they are good enough to make a living at it. Professional musicians can be found playing in concert halls, restaurants, and at parties.

A musician does not always work regular hours. Performances are often at night and on weekends. Some musicians work every day of the week. Musicians often tour from city to city or from country to country. These tours can last a year or more.

Justin sometimes visits schools and band camps to encourage young musicians.

Musicians 101

David Archuleta (1990–)

David started singing in public at the age of 10. He came to national attention when he appeared on *American Idol* in 2008. He was one of the youngest competitors ever. David finished as runner-up. In 2008, he released his first single "Crush" from his self-titled album. The album debuted at number two on the Billboard charts.

Nick Jonas (1992–)

Nick Jonas is one third of the musical group Jonas Brothers. He is a singer, songwriter, and actor. Nick made his Broadway debut at the age of seven. He appeared in many professional musicals, including *Les Miserables* and *The Sound of Music*. Nick and his brothers began touring as a group in 2005. Nick made his first television appearance with his brothers in an episode of *Hannah Montana*. His film debut followed in 2008 with the Disney Channel Original Movie called *Camp Rock*. In 2009, Nick formed the band Nick Jonas and the Administration. The band released its first album, Who I Am, in February 2010.

Taylor Swift (1989–)

Taylor is a country musician. She began her career when she was 11 years old, appearing at music venues in Nashville before catching the attention of record executives. In 2006, her self-titled album went multi-platinum. She had three smash singles from this album, "Tim McGraw," "Teardrops on My Guitar," and "Our Song." Taylor went on to win countless awards, including CMA Entertainer of the Year in 2009 and Best Female Video at the 2009 MTV Video Music Awards for "You Belong to Me."

Lea Michele Sarfati (1986–)

Lea is an actress and a singer born in New York City. She began working on Broadway at the age of eight. She appeared in *Les Miserables* and several other musicals. She earned a Drama Desk nomination for her leading role in *Spring Awakening*. Lea has become well-known for her role as Rachel Berry in the television series *Glee*. She received Emmy, Golden Globe, and Teen Choice Award nominations for this role. *Time* magazine included Michele in its 2010 list of 100 Most Influential People.

Microphones

When performing on stage, most musicians use microphones to make their music louder. Microphones turn sound into electrical signals that can be transmitted over distances. As well as a performance tool, microphones are used on radio and television shows and in recording studios.

Influences

Justin's mother, Pattie, worked hard to help Justin reach his dreams. She encouraged her son to pursue his love of music. Growing up, Justin listened to music by artists such as Stevie Wonder and R&B group Boyz II Men. Justin also credits Ne-Yo and Justin Timberlake as influences.

In many interviews, Justin has said that Michael Jackson was an inspiration to him. When he was younger, Justin would try to act and sing like Michael. He saw Michael as an entertainer and not just a dancer or a singer. Like Michael, Justin wants to put everything into his performances. He works hard to perfect his singing and dancing skills so that his fans enjoy his shows.

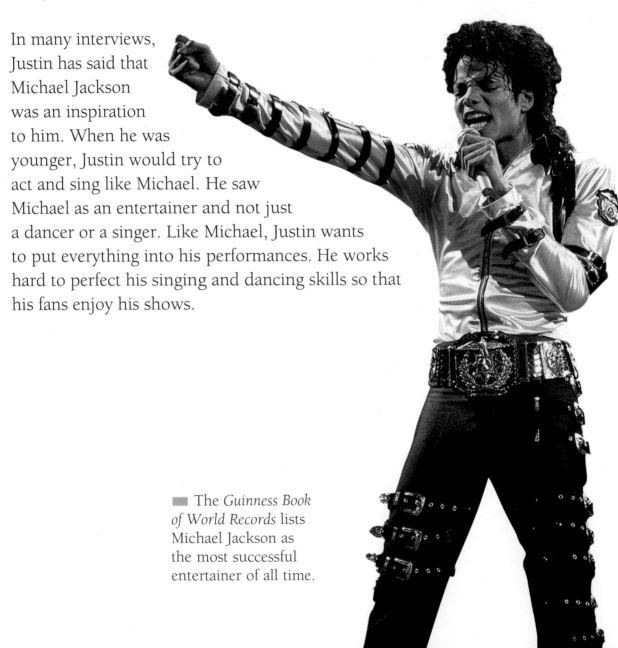

■ The *Guinness Book of World Records* lists Michael Jackson as the most successful entertainer of all time.

Usher has been a strong influence on Justin. Along with helping him get a recording contract, Usher has acted as a **mentor** to Justin. He has advised Justin on how to handle his fans and how to act in public. He has even helped Justin choose what types of clothing to wear and how to talk to interviewers.

THE BIEBER FAMILY

Justin lives mainly in Atlanta, Georgia, with his mother, but he still returns to Canada from time to time to visit friends and family. When in Canada, Justin often stays with his grandparents, who still live in Stratford. While there, he also visits his father, Jeremy.

Atlanta is Georgia's capital city. It is also the largest city in the state. Approximately 540,000 people live there.

Overcoming Obstacles

Growing up, Justin and his mother often struggled to make ends meet. According to Justin, not having as much as other people made him stronger. Justin worked hard on his musical skills. He practiced his drums and wrote songs.

When his friends were playing, Justin was happy to pick up his guitar. He would go to Stratford's Avon Theatre and **busk** on the theater's steps. Justin would earn $150 to $200 a day. This was enough to take his mother on their first trip ever. The pair headed off to Disney World.

■ Buskers perform in a variety of public places, such as subways, street corners, and parks.

When Justin signed his recording contract, he and his mother decided to move to Atlanta. They felt it would be best for his career if he were living in the United States near the music business. This was a hard decision for them to make. They had to leave behind family, friends, and everything they had known.

After his first single was released, Justin was still not well-known. He had to play in small venues across North America. Justin continued to work hard. He always took time to sign autographs and thank fans personally. He updated his Twitter account daily and continued to make YouTube videos. This allowed him to reach out to more people. When My World 2.0 debuted at number one, his fans were not surprised.

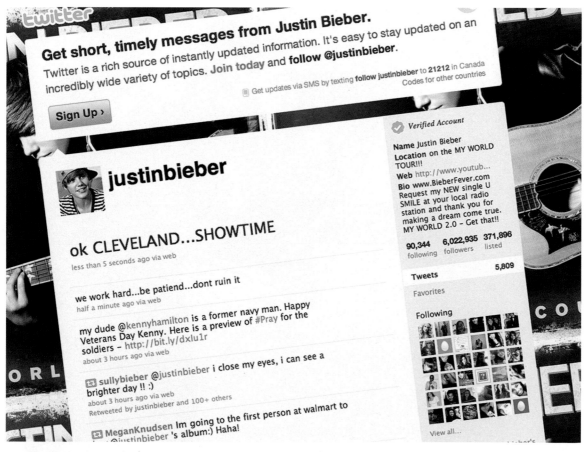

■ Justin has more than six million followers on Twitter.

Achievements and Successes

Due to his schedule, Justin does not attend a regular school. Instead, he is homeschooled by a tutor. His tutor even travels with Justin when he is on tour. Justin is a straight A student. He studies hard because he wants to go to college.

Justin's career has just begun, but he has had much success. When seven songs from his debut album made it onto the Billboard Top 100, people in the industry took notice of this talented performer. Some of the featured singles included "One Time," "One Less Lonely Girl," "Favorite Girl," and "Love Me." This was the first time in Billboard history that seven songs from a debut CD made the Billboard Hot 100.

Justin followed this success with the release of My World 2.0. When it debuted at number one on the charts, Justin became the youngest solo male artist to top the charts since Stevie Wonder in 1963. At one point in 2010, Justin had both the number one and number five albums.

■ While in Tokyo, Japan, in October 2010, Justin was presented with a gold record for record sales in Japan of more than 500,000 copies.

In 2010, Justin won big at the Teen Choice awards. Justin won for Choice Music: Breakout Artist–Male, Choice Male: Music, Choice Music: Pop Album, and Choice Summer: Music Star. In September 2010, he won his first MTV Video Music Award (VMA). He took home the Best New Artist VMA for his song "Baby."

HELPING OTHERS

Often, musicians use their popularity to increase public awareness of issues they care about. They may bring attention to environmental problems or organizations that are helping others. Justin has participated in several events that have drawn attention to special causes. In 2010, Justin took part in the recording of "We Are the World" to help the victims of the Haitian earthquake. He also participated in a telethon to help people affected by an oil spill in the Gulf of Mexico. Justin's fans helped him raise $200,000 in pennies for a children's hospital in Buffalo.

Justin is involved with several charities. One of these charities is called Pencils of Promise. This organization provides school supplies to communities around the world.

Write a Biography

A person's life story can be the subject of a book. This kind of book is called a biography. Biographies describe the lives of remarkable people, such as those who have achieved great success or have done important things to help others. These people may be alive today, or they may have lived many years ago. Reading a biography can help you learn more about a remarkable person.

At school, you might be asked to write a biography. First, decide who you want to write about. You can choose a musician, such as Justin Bieber, or any other person. Then, find out if your library has any books about this person. Learn as much as you can about him or her. Write down the key events in this person's life. What was this person's childhood like? What has he or she accomplished? What are his or her goals? What makes this person special or unusual?

A concept web is a useful research tool. Read the questions in the following concept web. Answer the questions in your notebook. Your answers will help you write a biography.

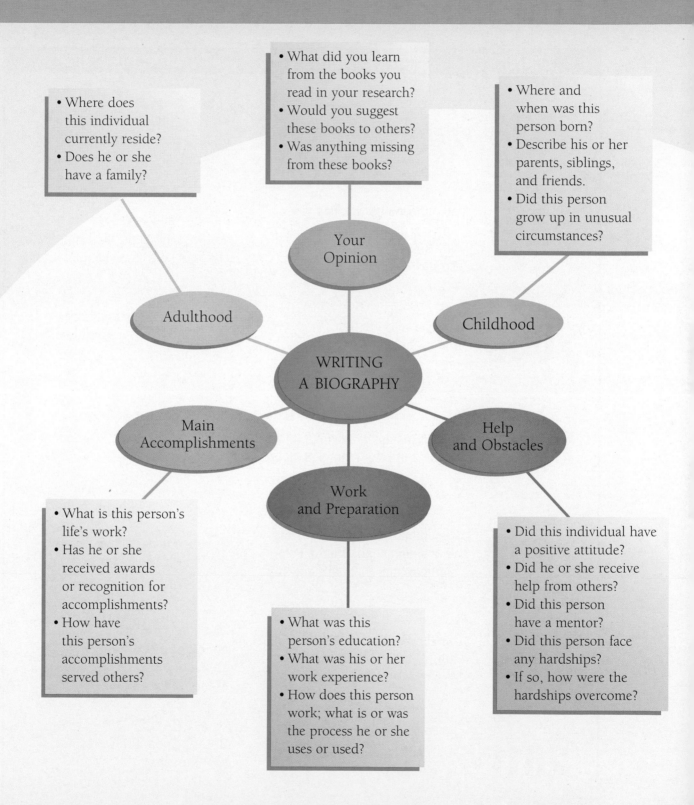

- Where does this individual currently reside?
- Does he or she have a family?

- What did you learn from the books you read in your research?
- Would you suggest these books to others?
- Was anything missing from these books?

- Where and when was this person born?
- Describe his or her parents, siblings, and friends.
- Did this person grow up in unusual circumstances?

Your Opinion

Adulthood

Childhood

WRITING A BIOGRAPHY

Main Accomplishments

Help and Obstacles

Work and Preparation

- What is this person's life's work?
- Has he or she received awards or recognition for accomplishments?
- How have this person's accomplishments served others?

- What was this person's education?
- What was his or her work experience?
- How does this person work; what is or was the process he or she uses or used?

- Did this individual have a positive attitude?
- Did he or she receive help from others?
- Did this person have a mentor?
- Did this person face any hardships?
- If so, how were the hardships overcome?

Timeline

YEAR	JUSTIN BIEBER	WORLD EVENTS
1994	Justin Bieber is born on March 1.	"I Will Always Love You," by Whitney Houston, is awarded Record of the Year at the Grammys.
2007	Justin's mother posts a video on YouTube of him performing at a singing competition in Stratford, Ontario.	Rihanna and Jay-Z win Best Video of the Year for "Umbrella" at the MTV Video Music Awards.
2008	Justin lands his first recording contract.	Michael Jackson's Thriller album is re-released for its 25th anniversary.
2009	Justin releases his debut album, My World, which goes platinum.	Fearless by Taylor Swift is the top-selling album.
2009	Justin makes Billboard history with seven songs from a debut album on the Billboard Top 100.	Beyoncé is named Woman of the Year by Billboard.
2010	Justin wins Best New Artist at the MTV Video Music Awards.	Musicians gather to perform on the Hope for Haiti telethon, an event that helped victims of the Haiti earthquake.
2011	A 3D movie about Justin's life is released.	Britney Spears releases her seventh album.

Words to Know

agent: a person who finds talent for the entertainment industry and helps talent find jobs that suit their skills

album: a collection of songs released in one package, such as a CD

Billboard: charts produced by a weekly magazine that rate the popularity of music

busk: to entertain on a street or public place for money

debut: a first appearance or presentation

demos: trial recordings of songs or an album that are used to attract interest from record companies, musicians, and other artists

executive: senior management of a company

mentor: someone who offers advice to a less experienced person

percussion: the striking of an instrument to produce tones

platinum: an award given to a musical artist who sells one million units of an album

R&B: rhythm and blues; a style of music

single: a song sent out for radio stations to play

Index

Log on to www.av2books.com

AV² by Weigl brings you media enhanced books that support active learning. Go to www.av2books.com, and enter the special code found on page 2 of this book. You will gain access to enriched and enhanced content that supplements and complements this book. Content includes video, audio, web links, quizzes, a slide show, and activities.

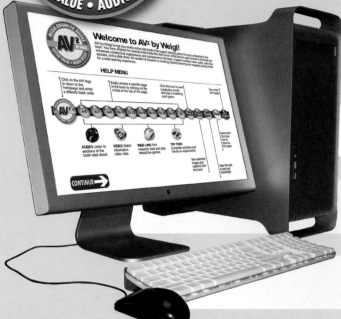

Audio
Listen to sections of the book read aloud.

Video
Watch informative video clips.

Embedded Weblinks
Gain additional information for research.

Try This!
Complete activities and hands-on experiments.

WHAT'S ONLINE?

Try This!	Embedded Weblinks	Video	EXTRA FEATURES
Complete an activity about your childhood.	Learn more about Justin Bieber's life.	Watch a video about Justin Bieber.	**Audio** Listen to sections of the book read aloud.
Try this activity about key events.	More information on Justin Bieber's achievments and awards.	Check out another video about Justin Bieber.	
Complete an activity about overcoming obstacles.	Check out a site about Justin Bieber.		**Key Words** Study vocabulary, and complete a matching word activity.
Write a biography.			
Try this timeline activity.			**Slide Show** View images and captions, and prepare a presentation.
			Quizzes Test your knowledge.

AV² was built to bridge the gap between print and digital. We encourage you to tell us what you like and what you want to see in the future.

Sign up to be an AV² Ambassador at www.av2books.com/ambassador.